BEI GRIN MACHT SICH IHR WISSEN BEZAHLT

- Wir veröffentlichen Ihre Hausarbeit, Bachelor- und Masterarbeit
- Ihr eigenes eBook und Buch - weltweit in allen wichtigen Shops
- Verdienen Sie an jedem Verkauf

Jetzt bei www.GRIN.com hochladen und kostenlos publizieren

Bibliografische Information der Deutschen Nationalbibliothek:

Die Deutsche Bibliothek verzeichnet diese Publikation in der Deutschen Nationalbibliografie; detaillierte bibliografische Daten sind im Internet über http://dnb.d-nb.de/ abrufbar.

Dieses Werk sowie alle darin enthaltenen einzelnen Beiträge und Abbildungen sind urheberrechtlich geschützt. Jede Verwertung, die nicht ausdrücklich vom Urheberrechtsschutz zugelassen ist, bedarf der vorherigen Zustimmung des Verlages. Das gilt insbesondere für Vervielfältigungen, Bearbeitungen, Übersetzungen, Mikroverfilmungen, Auswertungen durch Datenbanken und für die Einspeicherung und Verarbeitung in elektronische Systeme. Alle Rechte, auch die des auszugsweisen Nachdrucks, der fotomechanischen Wiedergabe (einschließlich Mikrokopie) sowie der Auswertung durch Datenbanken oder ähnliche Einrichtungen, vorbehalten.

Impressum:

Copyright © 2010 GRIN Verlag
Druck und Bindung: Books on Demand GmbH, Norderstedt Germany
ISBN: 9783668648623

Dieses Buch bei GRIN:

https://www.grin.com/document/413461

James Pinnock

Sultan Saladin as the liberator of Jerusalem?

GRIN Verlag

GRIN - Your knowledge has value

Der GRIN Verlag publiziert seit 1998 wissenschaftliche Arbeiten von Studenten, Hochschullehrern und anderen Akademikern als eBook und gedrucktes Buch. Die Verlagswebsite www.grin.com ist die ideale Plattform zur Veröffentlichung von Hausarbeiten, Abschlussarbeiten, wissenschaftlichen Aufsätzen, Dissertationen und Fachbüchern.

Besuchen Sie uns im Internet:

http://www.grin.com/

http://www.facebook.com/grincom

http://www.twitter.com/grin_com

ASSESS SALAH' AL-DIN'S ACHIEVEMENTS

It is, according to A. R. Azzam, only "by putting Jerusalem aside [that] we can catch a glimpse of the real Saladin".[1] Should we therefore, as Andrew Ehrenkreutz suggests, question whether history would view Saladin in the same manner if he had died in 1185, or does this unduly undermine the historical importance of events in 1187? Even in its centrality to Saladin's career and legacy, Hattin represents just one of many of Saladin's notable achievements: "The liberator of Jerusalem, a chivalrous knight, a generous benefactor, [and] a political upstart".[2] There are evidently a multitude of mediums in which one can interpret Saladin's career and achievements: his contemporary chroniclers saw him as the champion of Muslim holy war, with the pinnacle of his career arriving with his victory at Hattin; A. R. Azzam sees Saladin's defining success in the context of the Sunni Revival, and suggests his greatest achievement was the restoration of Sunni Islam into Fatimid Egypt; others, such as Ehrenkreutz and Tyerman, see Saladin as a scheming politician seeking personal aggrandizement who manipulated the 'fluidity and opportunities' of Near Eastern politics in the twelfth century.[3] This essay will firstly examine the chronicles of Imad al-Din al-Isfahani and Baha ad-Din Ibn Shaddad, which establish *jihad* and the Counter-Crusade as the most important aspect of Saladin's career, as do the majority of modern historians.[4] However, by shifting the focus away from Hattin and Jerusalem, from the *Dar al-Harb* towards the *Dar al-Islam*, and furthermore by examining the less laudatory assessments of Saladin, this essay will attempt to reach a more balanced and extensive assessment of Saladin's achievements.[5]

Many have seen Saladin as the 'spiritual son' of Nur al-Din, under whose rule the counter-crusade was born. Indeed, Bonner suggests that Saladin's achievements represent the

---

[1] A. R. Azzam, *Saladin* (Harlow, 2009), p. 6. For the purpose of this essay I will use the more Westernized and Anglicized spelling of Salah' al-Din's name.

[2] Ibid., p. 2.

[3] Christopher Tyerman, *God's War: A New History of the Crusades* (London, 2007), p. 350.

[4] Donald S. Richards, 'Imad al-Din al-Isfahani: Administrator, Litterateur and Historian' in Maya Shatzmiller (ed.), *Crusaders and Muslims in Twelfth-Century Syria* (Leiden, 1993), p. 144.

[5] Peter Lock, *The Routledge Companion to the Crusades* (London, 2006), p. 415.

"culmination of three generations' effort in the Counter-Crusade".[6] Nikita Elisséeff sets out the four aims of Nur al-Din in the 'domain' of the Counter-Crusade: the revival of jihad, the liberation of Jerusalem, the establishment of the political unity of Islam, and the diffusion of the Muslim ideology.[7] The Muslim scholar al-Sulami (d. 1106) in his *Kitab al-Jihad* warned the Muslims "Know for certain that this enemy's attack on your country, and their achieving what they have over some of you is a warning from God (who is praised) to those of you that remain".[8] He advocated that the success of the Christians in the First Crusade was a symptom of the moral and political decay of Islam. Nur al-Din's Counter-Crusade was certainly borne from al-Sulami's harangue, and an examination of Saladin's career certainly paints him as the very answer to al-Sulami's exhortation. This very idea of Saladin as the champion of the Counter-Crusade and Muslim holy war is epitomized by the work of Baha ad-Din Ibn Shaddad, who writes that "the sultan entertained an ardent passion for the holy war; his mind was always filled with it".[9] Indeed, later in the work Baha ad-Din states that "His desire to fight in God's cause forced him to leave his family, his children, his native land, the place of his abode, and all else in his land".[10] Although it is almost certain that this is a literary hyperbole, devised to further glorify Saladin as a *mujahid*, it does portray Saladin was seen first a champion of jihad, second a ruler of lands, reflecting his centrality to the Counter-Crusade rhetoric of the mid- to late- twelfth century.

Saladin's crowning achievement in the Counter-Crusade was his victory over the forces of Jerusalem at the Horns of Hattin in 1187. Saladin's chronicler and personal confidant, Imad al-Din al–Isfahani, whose works witness according to Donald Richards the "partnership between Imad al-Din's pen and the Sultan's sword", give us key insight into the impact of Saladin's victory and Hattin.[11] Indeed, the very fact that Richard's uses such a con-

---

[6] Michael Bonner, *Jihad in Islamic History* (Princeton, 2006), p. 142.

[7] Nikita Elisséeff, 'The Reaction of the Syrian Muslims after the Foundation of the First Latin Kingdom of Jerusalem' in Maya Shatzmiller (ed.), *Crusaders and Muslims in Twelfth-Century Syria* (Leiden, 1993), p. 167.

[8] Niall Christie, 'A Translation of Extracts from the Kitab al-Jihad of 'Ali ibn Tahir Al-Sulami (d. 1106)', 2001 http://www.arts.cornell.edu/prh3/447/texts/Sulami.html (viewed 11. Jan 2010).

[9] 'Baha ad-Din's *Life of Saladin*' in Allen, S. J. and Emilie Ant (eds.), *The Crusades: A Reader* (Peterborough, Ontario, 2003), p. 150.

[10] Ibid., pp. 150-1.

[11] Richards, 'Imad al-Din al-Isfahani', p. 144.

cept as an alliance between the scholar's pen and the Sultan's sword reflects the very fact that in contemporary scholarship, Saladin is primarily seen as the conquering hero of Muslim holy war, with his place in history irrevocably linked with his military victories. This is, unsurprisingly, the view of Saladin by Imad al-Din also, who summarizes the events of the battle, recording how,

"he [Saladin] cut off their access to water and filled in the wells, which caused them great hardships. He prevented their getting down to the water and put himself between them and their objective, keeping them at a distance … on a burningly hot day".[12]

This quotation not only reveals Imad al-Din's appreciation of Saladin's skills of military leadership, but attributes the victory solely to Saladin, establishing him (as he does throughout his chronicle) as the champion of jihad. Indeed, in his 'Hattin letter', more of a triumph song than a battlefield communiqué according to Melville and Lyons, Saladin proclaims after the battle that "the domain of Islam has expanded … the gleam of God's sword has terrified the polytheists".[13] Clearly, the victory at Hattin symbolized for the Muslims not only a momentous victory in the Counter-Crusade, but as fulfilling what Imad al-Din terms "just vengeance".[14]

In the 'afterglow' of Hattin, Saladin went on to conquer the entire Kingdom of Jerusalem, apart from the coastal city of Tyre.[15] Although the Third Crusade stretched Muslim resources to their very limit, and represents somewhat of a disappointing denouement to Saladin's career, through his diplomacy with Richard I, Saladin managed to retain all the Muslim territories apart from Ascalon and Jaffa. However, as A. R. Azzam suggests, it is hard to exaggerate the scale of Saladin's victory at Hattin which witnessed the devastation of the entire Christian army and the entire Kingdom of Jerusalem in one day.[16] It is this victory that estab-

---

[12] *Arab historians of the Crusades*, tr. Francesco Gabrieli (London, 1969), p. 131.

[13] C. P. Melville and M. C. Lyons, 'Saladin's Hattin Letter' in B. Z. Kedar (ed.), *The Horns of Hattin* (Jerusalem, 1992), pp. 208-10.

[14] *Arab historians of the Crusades*, tr. Francesco Gabrieli (London, 1969), p. 129.

[15] Carole Hillenbrand, *The Crusades: Islamic perspectives* (Edinburgh, 1999), p. 180.

lished the legend of Saladin as the "conquering hero" of Muslim holy war and cemented his place in history.[17]

When we examine Hattin through the rather Westernized view of the Crusades, we see only Saladin's military success in the Counter-Crusade. If we put aside Jerusalem as A. R. Azzam suggests, we may see that the greatest achievement of Saladin at the battle of Hattin was not his momentous victory in the Counter-Crusade, but rather that he succeeded in gathering the largest Muslim army since the Abbasid times, an army held together by the sheer force of Saladin's personality.[18] "On its march its dust darkened the sun", Saladin proudly boasted of his Muslim army, which comprised contingents from Egypt, Iraq, Damascus, Aleppo, Mosul, Sinjar, Nisbin, Amid, Irbil and Diyar Bakr.[19] Saladin was able to use his diplomatic and political skills, perhaps his "doggedness" as Azzam suggests, to unite Egypt, Syria and Palestine under the banner of Sunni Islam, and under his personal rule and leadership.[20] Yet this is according to some historians where the 'legend' of Saladin comes undone. Far from the master tactician and diplomat who united Islam to defeat the infidel Frank, Lyons and Jackson suggest that Saladin was "a dynast who used Islam for his own purposes", a view shared by other historians as we shall now see.[21]

Robert Irwin suggests that there are two aspects to the greater part of Saladin's career: first, his various unsuccessful attempts to take Mosul from the Zengids; and second, his drive to create an empire.[22] In fact, it was not until 1187 that Saladin fought a Christian army, before this he had fought only his Muslim neighbors. According to Saladin, however, in his many letters to the caliph, Holy War could not be fought effectively without the Zengid-

---

[16] Azzam, *Saladin*, p. 181.

[17] H. A. R. Gibb, *The Life of Saladin: From the works of Imad ad-Din and Baha ad-Din* (Oxford, 1973), p. 1.

[18] Azzam, *Saladin*, pp. 179-80.

[19] Ibid., p. 170.

[20] Azzam, *Saladin*, p. 237.

[21] Carole Hillenbrand, *The Crusades: Islamic perspectives* (Edinburgh, 1999), p. 185.

[22] Robert Irwin, 'Islam and the Crusades 1096-1699' in Jonathan Riley-Smith (ed.), *The Oxford History of the Crusades* (Oxford, 2002), p. 228.

controlled Mosul and Aleppo: for jihad, Syria had to be the centre of his empire.[23] Therefore, we are forced to question whether Saladin, in his persistent aim to conquer Syria, represents a 'champion of jihad' or a 'warlord usurper'. In fact, Carole Hillenbrand suggests that Saladin justified his actions retrospectively in terms of jihad. To what extent, however, can a policy of conquest and political *quid pro quo* between Saladin and his fellow Sunni Muslims which lasted over a decade be explained and justified by Saladin's promise to the caliph of jihad? According to Ehrenkreutz, Saladin's policy was not one ultimately driven by Holy War and the Counter-Crusade, but ultimately by his own personal agenda. Indeed, Ehrenkreutz sees Saladin as a master-puppeteer of 'unscrupulous schemes' for personal aggrandizement, and suggests that this is how he would have been remembered had he died in 1185.[24] The German historian Köhler shares a similar sentiment, arguing that Saladin's treaty with Raymond of Tripoli in the year preceding Hattin displays a severe lack of scruples, in contradicting his own 'ardent passion' for just vengeance and jihad against the Christian enemy.[25] Nevertheless, the fact remains that Saladin built an empire during his lifetime, almost seamlessly it seems, that according to Christopher Tyerman, made him "the effective overlord of the Fertile Crescent".[26] Although it is certainly contestable that Saladin aimed to build an empire, it seems that he did indeed have jihad in mind, although it perhaps became too easy a retrospective justification for his actions against his fellow Muslims as Hillenbrand suggests.

Let us not forget, however, that Saladin was a man motivated by religion. According to Baha ad-Din "Whenever he heard the Koran, his heart was touched and his eyes would fill with tears on most occasions".[27] Indeed, Saladin was a 'child of the Sunni Revival', his greatest achievement, according to A. R. Azzam, arriving in 1171 with the restoration of Sunni Islam into Fatimid Shi'ite Egypt.[28] The construction of *madrasas* became the primary mode of transmitting the message of the Sunni Revival. Beginning under Nur al-Din, and cultivated under Saladin, through the jurists, the *madrasa* became the main weapon to spread

---

[23] Azzam, *Saladin*, p. 155.

[24] Hillenbrand, *The Crusades: Islamic perspectives*, p. 185.

[25] Ibid., p. 185.

[26] Tyerman, *God's War*, p. 350.

[27] Ibn Shaddad, *The Rare and Excellent History of Saladin*, trans. D. S. Richards (Aldershot, 2001), p. 20.

[28] Azzam, *Saladin*, p. 7.

the message of the Counter-Crusade. Indeed, Azzam proposes that under Saladin occurred "the birth of an army of ulama", whereby the message of the Sunni Revival was carried into battle.[29] Thus the madrasa became an ideological foundation for the success of Saladin's Counter-Crusade. Furthermore, the function of the madrasa was, as Irwin suggests, to foster orthodoxy, as it did in Egypt.[30] Wiet offers another aspect to this view of the function of the madrasa, claiming that the system of madrasas created by Saladin throughout Egypt and Syria created an 'intellectual homogeneity' which allowed for, and nurtured, the unity of Islam against the Christian enemy.[31] The scale of Saladin's policy of Sunnification is emphasized by the legacy of madrasas he left: by 1193, Damascus boasted thirty madrasas, and by the mid-thirteenth century Cairo and Fustat had thirty-two between them. Upon his entry into Jerusalem in 1187, according to Imad al-Din, Saladin "set aside for the use of the *madrasa* the church dedicated to St John near the Gate of the Tribes … He also set aside sites for *madrasas* for the various (other) communities".[32] Thus, it seems that Saladin's conquests were not merely an act of material and military expansion, but a means by which to transmit the ideas of the Sunni Revival, which provided the basis for Saladin's achievement of the uniformity of Islam and the revival of jihad.

Should we therefore, in order to gain a more enlightened assessment of Saladin's achievements, suppose that Saladin had not lived until 1187? It is clear that one cannot remove one of the greatest of Saladin's achievements for the sake of an argument. This amounts to no more than historical amputation. As Hillenbrand rightly points out, Baha ad-Din does not devote the largest part of his biography to the last six years of Saladin's life (1187-93) for no reason at all.[33] Furthermore, it seems that Ehrenkreutz in his wish to malign Saladin as a 'warlord usurper' falls prey to hyperbole, and exaggerates the extent of Saladin's conflicts against his fellow Muslims. Furthermore, Ehrenkreutz and Tyerman are wrongly concerned more with Saladin's motives, rather than his achievements. One cannot deny the magnitude and very scale of Saladin's achievements: he united Islam both militarily and

---

[29] Ibid., p. 42.

[30] Irwin, 'Islam and the Crusades 1096-1699', p. 228.

[31] Azzam, *Saladin*, p. 136.

[32] *Arab historians of the Crusades*, tr. Francesco Gabrieli (London, 1969), p. 174.

[33] Hillenbrand, *The Crusades: Islamic perspectives*, p. 180.

ideologically, he regained Jerusalem and retook control of the Levant, crushing the Crusaders and preventing their ever regaining a substantial foothold in the Near East. It is, however, Egypt which represents the greatest of his achievements. Not merely, as Azzam suggests, by his restoration of Sunni Islam to the very heart of the Fatimid empire, but more so because it provided the very foundations for his success in the Counter-Crusade. As the Templars repeatedly advocated, "though the prize of the struggle was Jerusalem, the key was Egypt".[34] Without his success in Egypt, it is doubtful that Saladin would have met with such success later in his career. Without Egypt, the legend of Saladin would never have been born.

---

[34] Azzam, *Saladin*, p. 240.

Bibliography

Primary Material

Arab historians of the Crusades, tr. Francesco Gabrieli (London, 1969).

'Baha ad-Din's *Life of Saladin*' in Allen, S. J. and Emilie Ant (eds.), *The Crusades: A Reader* (Peterborough, Ontario, 2003), pp. 148-153.

Christie, Niall, 'A Translation of Extracts from the Kitab al-Jihad of 'Ali ibn Tahir Al-Sulami (d. 1106)', 2001 http://www.arts.cornell.edu/prh3/447/texts/Sulami.html (viewed 11. Jan 2010).

Melville, C. P. and M. C. Lyons, 'Saladin's Hattin Letter' in B. Z. Kedar (ed.), *The Horns of Hattin* (Jerusalem, 1992), pp. 208-12.

Ibn Shaddad, *The Rare and Excellent History of Saladin*, trans. D. S. Richards (Aldershot, 2001).

Secondary Material

Azzam, A. R., *Saladin* (Harlow, 2009).

Bonner, Michael, *Jihad in Islamic History* (Princeton, 2006).

Ehrenkreutz, Andrew S., 'The Crisis of the Dinar in the Egypt of Saladin', *Journal of the American Oriental Society*, Vol. 76, No. 3 (Jul. – Sep., 1956), pp. 178-184.

Elisséeff, Nikita, 'The Reaction of the Syrian Muslims after the Foundation of the First Latin Kingdom of Jerusalem' in Maya Shatzmiller (ed.), *Crusaders and Muslims in Twelfth-Century Syria* (Leiden, 1993), pp. 162-72.

Gibb, H. A. R., *The Life of Saladin: From the works of Imad ad-Din and Baha ad-Din* (Oxford, 1973).

Hillenbrand, Carole, *The Crusades: Islamic perspectives* (Edinburgh, 1999).

Irwin, Robert, 'Islam and the Crusades 1096-1699' in Jonathan Riley-Smith (ed.), *The Oxford History of the Crusades* (Oxford, 2002), pp. 211-57.

Lock, Peter, *The Routledge Companion to the Crusades* (London, 2006).

Richards, Donald S., 'Imad al-Din al-Isfahani: Administrator, Litterateur and Historian' in Maya Shatzmiller (ed.), *Crusaders and Muslims in Twelfth-Century Syria* (Leiden, 1993), pp. 133-46.

Tyerman, Christopher, *God's War: A New History of the Crusades* (London, 2007).

BEI GRIN MACHT SICH IHR WISSEN BEZAHLT

- Wir veröffentlichen Ihre Hausarbeit, Bachelor- und Masterarbeit

- Ihr eigenes eBook und Buch - weltweit in allen wichtigen Shops

- Verdienen Sie an jedem Verkauf

Jetzt bei www.GRIN.com hochladen und kostenlos publizieren